The Scottish
Limerick Book

BY THE SAME AUTHOR

The Great British Limerick Book – Filthy Limericks for (Nearly) Every Town in the UK

ALSO BY THE SAME AUTHOR (BUT ABSOLUTELY, CATEGORICALLY NOTHING REMOTELY LIKE THIS BOOK OR THE GREAT BRITISH LIMERICK BOOK)

Scott Walker: The Rhymes of Goodbye

A Generation of Change, a Lifetime of Difference? British Social Policy since 1979 (with Martin Evans)

The Scottish Limerick Book

Filthy Limericks for Every Town in Scotland

Lewis Williams

CORONA
BOOKS

First published in the United Kingdom in 2015
Reprinted with minor revisions 2016

By Corona Books UK

www.coronabooks.com

The verse in this volume is a greatly expanded
version of material previously published as part of
The Great British Limerick Book by Lewis Williams
(Corona Books UK, 2015).

ISBN 978-0-9932472-1-7

Cover design by Colourburst
www.colourburst.com

INTRODUCTION

Have you ever wanted to see a filthy limerick for virtually every town in Scotland? You have?! Your dreams have just come true. *The Scottish Limerick Book* is intended to be comprehensive and include a limerick for every city and all but the smallest towns in the country. However, as there is no legal definition of what does or doesn't constitute a town in Scotland – for when a village is not a village and big enough to be a town, or for when a suburb is not just a suburb and separate enough to be a town in its own right – I've tried to cast the net reasonably wide and ensure that a limerick is included in some way for every settlement which, according to the General Register Office for Scotland's mid-2012 population estimates, has a population of 3,000 or more. Although this is a completely arbitrary figure, it seemed as sensible a cut-off point to choose as any. It means that a number of larger villages (those with a population over 3,000) get a limerick here. A number of smaller places do also get a limerick too, especially those that have been identified as towns or are former burghs or, let's be honest, have names that make for good words to rhyme with. If I've missed out your town or anywhere else out that I should have included according to the above criteria, then the mistake is all mine and apologies are due. (Or perhaps you're grateful!) I've also tried to make every effort to capture the correct pronunciation of place names, but again if there are genuine mistakes (as opposed to what I like to think of as inventive rhyming as in, say, the limerick for Kingussie) then the fault is mine and apologies are due. Complaints and/or praise can be heaped on me via the website for the book, and will reach me.

In a small number of occasional instances in the book, where a traditional or anonymous limerick already existed for a town or where an existing limerick fitted well for a town, the anonymous/traditional verse is used. All these instances are marked with an asterisk next to the place name. All the rest of this is, for better or for worse, my own work. Some of the limericks in the book, particularly those for larger towns and cities, were previously published as part of my *The Great British Limerick Book*, but this is very much an independent book for Scotland. There are more new limericks in this book than there are old. I hope you enjoy them.

Lewis Williams

CONTENTS

Limericks from ...

Aberdeen and Aberdeenshire   1
Angus and Dundee   12
Argyll and Bute   17
Clackmannanshire   21
Dumfries and Galloway   25
East Ayrshire   31
East Dunbartonshire   36
East Lothian   41
East Renfrewshire   45
Falkirk   48
Fife   53
Highland   65
Inverclyde and Glasgow   74
Midlothian and Edinburgh   78
Moray   83
North Ayrshire   88
North Lanarkshire   94
Perth and Kinross   102
Renfrewshire   106
Scottish Borders   111
Shetland and Orkney   118
South Ayrshire   120
South Lanarkshire   123
Stirling   132
West Dunbartonshire   135
West Lothian   139
Western Isles   145

Index of Towns   148

Note: Limericks that are marked with an asterisk are traditional/anonymous in authorship or adapted from traditional or anonymous rhymes. All other limericks copyright Lewis Williams 2016.

Aberdeen and Aberdeenshire

Aberdeen*

A young man from Aberdeen, he
Once spilt gin all over his weenie
Just to be couth
He added vermouth
And slipped his girlfriend a martini

Banchory

At the doctor's surgery in Banch-ory
I said, 'I'll try to cut short a long story
I was shagging the life
Out of the fishmonger's wife
And he's shoved up my arse a John Dory†'

Banff

Near Banff's most picturesque bay
I went to a fancy soirée
Where it was a social clanger
To get out my wanger
Even if it was only half way

---

† A John Dory, in case a definition is required, is an edible marine fish with rather large spikes on its fins.

Dyce

Said this young lady I met in Dyce
'Come to bed with me. It'll be nice
There's really no place finer
Than near my vagina
Just ask all of my pubic lice'

Ellon

There was a young lady from Ellon
Who had one most enormous melon
So her other breast
Was quite second best
And didn't look much like a well 'un

Fraserburgh

Fraserburgh is known for its shellfish
But when I screwed there this lady called Trish
The crabs that I caught
Were not of the sort
You would serve in a fine dining dish

Huntly

I was driving in the town of Huntly
When the driver behind me did shunt me
I was fairly surprised
But he apologised
Saying, 'I'm sorry, I'm a right cunt, me'

Inverurie

Once in the town of Inverurie
I was wanking away with a fury
On the top deck of a bus
Which caused quite a fuss
And I ended up facing a jury

Kemnay

In Highland dress a chap in Kem-nay
Broke wind as he knelt down to pray
To add to his guilt
The blast raised his kilt
And left his bare arse on display

Kingswells

A husband and wife from Kingswells
Were parted and so legend tells
The grounds for divorce
Were his farts of such force
The loudest at ten decibels

Kintore

A young lady from the town of Kintore
Excused herself from the dancefloor
Saying, 'I won't dance tonight
My bra's not quite right
It holds my tits most insecure'

Macduff

This lovely young lady from Macduff
Inspired me to write poems and stuff
About her retroussé nose
And her delicate toes
But most of all praising her muff

Newtonhill

At this restaurant in Newtonhill
I said, 'Your food's only fit for pig swill
In my stew I found blubber
And someone's used rubber
At least knock a quid off the bill'

Oldmeldrum

Said a young man from Oldmel-drum
'I must make this a new rule of thumb
For both me and my gerbil
It's more comforterbil‡
If I stop sticking him up my bum'

Peterculter

Said a young lady from Peterculter§
Thinking a cheap dildo just wouldn't suit her:
'I must try to get hold
Of one made from gold
Or I'll settle for one made of pewter'

---

‡ Which was naturally how he pronounced the word
'comfortable'!
§ Which is pronounced 'Peter-cooter'

Peterhead

Once in the town of Peterhead
I was wanking away in this bed
But it was on the top floor
Of a furniture store
And again to my arrest this led

Portlethen

And one time in Portlethen town
I was stroking my dick up and down
In a branch of Barclays Bank
But was arrested mid-wank
Which quite changed my smile to a frown

Stonehaven

One time in the town of Stonehaven
I gave into this curious craving
And started pulling my pud
In the middle of a pub
And was cautioned for such misbehaving

Turriff

To his girlfriend a chap from Turriff
Said, 'I'm sorry my dick's not so stiff
It was alright last night
When I turned out the light
And snuggled up with my German Mastiff††'

---

†† That is the breed of dog more commonly known as the
Great Dane.

Westhill

A man to his wife from Westhill
Said, 'I'm worried you don't trust me still
And it's rather a meanness
To have chopped off my penis
Just 'cause I smiled at your sister Jill'

Angus and Dundee

Arbroath

A vicar there was from Arbroath
Was once heard to mutter an oath
When attacked by some badgers
That went for his nadgers
And unfortunately bit off them both

Brechin

I addressed thus a meeting in Brechin†:
'Unaccustomed I am to public speaking
And I can't explain why
I've left open my fly
And my penis is out of it peeking'

Carnoustie

In the small Scottish town of Carnoustie
To some strange habits they introduced me
I'd never seen such a thing
As their bondage sling
And to tears I admit it reduced me

---

† Pronounced with a long 'e', hence 'Breekin'

Dundee*

There was an old man from Dundee
Who had sex with an ape in a tree
The results were quite horrid
All ass and no forehead
Three balls and a purple goatee

Forfar

To the doctor I said, 'It's pathetic
Those pills were a strong diuretic
I don't mean to be quibbling
But I've not seen such bad dribbling
Since I last watched Forfar Athletic'

Kirriemuir

There was a chap from Kirriemuir
Who covered his dick in manure
In the hope it would grow
If he treated it so
But it just rather marred its allure

Monifieth

A young lady from Monifieth
Told me something quite beyond belief
That her vagina could speak
Well, I gave it a week
But all I heard from it was a queef

Montrose

There was an old man from Montrose
Who quite often his dick would expose
Especially when swimming
He'd annoy all the women
By pulling up and down his Speedos

Stobswell

I asked the doctor from Stobswell
If he could tell me if my Uncle Bob's well
He said for an answer
'It's testicular cancer
But on the positive side, though, his knob's well'

Argyll and Bute

Campbeltown

In Campbeltown, where they make whisky
I had an obvious affair that was risky
When her husband caught us
He said, 'I won't make a fuss
But can I join in 'cause I'm frisky?'

Dunoon

One December near the town of Dunoon
I joined in with a nudist commune
But it was hardly the weather
For the altogether
And my balls shrivelled up like dried prunes

Helensburgh

From Helensburgh once I went sailing
With a lass whose love was unfailing
But her grip was so strong
As she played with my dong
That I spent the whole afternoon wailing

ARGYLL AND BUTE

Inveraray

One night a chap from Inveraray
Reported to A&E, slightly wary:
'I was alone having fun
And I've got stuck up my bum
Two aubergines and a canary'

Lochgilphead

With my lady friend from Lochgilphead
I said, 'Must you eat breakfast in bed?
Just look at my plums
They're all covered in crumbs
And in my bum crack there's stuck some fried bread'

Oban

There was once a survey in Oban†
Sexual habits it did have a probe on
The respondent most rum
Was the chap who couldn't come
Without his ecclesiastical robe on

Rothesay

An old man from Rothesay, Bute
Did his laundry in his birthday suit
Till he let his dick dangle
And it went in the mangle
And caused him a pain quite acute

---

† Pronounced 'Obe-an'

Clackmannanshire

Alloa

There was a young lady from Alloa
Whose boyfriend was a famous fruit grower
She bragged to her chums
About the size of his plums
And the stalk that he'd quite often show her

Alva

I complained at the sex shop in Alva†:
'Don't give me all of this palaver
I wanted a finely made
Masturbation aid
And you've sold me a hollowed out guava'

Clackmannan

'My perversions,' said a chap from Clackmannan
'Of taste and decency break every canon
At the butchers yet again
I was asked to refrain
From rubbing my dick with their gammon'

---

† Here as elsewhere in the book a slight bit of artistic licence is employed. There isn't really a sex shop in Alva, or if there is I haven't found it and I'm sure its products are of the highest quality.

Muckhart

An explosion occurred in Muckhart
When a camper set light to a fart
And was so flatulent
It blew up his tent
Then tore the whole campsite apart

Tillicoultry

I met this chap in Tillicoultry‡
When the weather was quite hot and sultry
And I was feeling randy
So it was very handy
When his wife offered me some adultery

---

‡ Pronounced 'Til-lee-coo-tee', which is nevertheless (I think!?)
a near (enough) rhyme with sultry and adultery. Send in your
complaints to the usual address.

Tullibody

There was a young man from Tullibody
Whose habits were really quite odd, he
Could only get aroused
If he put on a blouse
And listened to Showaddywaddy

Dumfries and Galloway

Annan*

There once was a young man from Annan
Who was blown down the street by a cannon
The force of the blast
Blew his balls up his ass
And his penis to the River Shannon

Castle Douglas*

A young lady from Castle Douglas
Used a dynamite stick as a phallus
They found her vagina
In North Carolina
And her arsehole in Buckingham Palace

Dalbeattie

There was a young lady from Dalbeattie
Who according to local graffiti
She had no holes barred
If you had some lard
And promised to call her a sweetie

Dumfries*

There was a young lady from Dumfries
Whose muff hair hung down to her knees
The crabs in her mott
Tied the hair in a knot
And constructed a flying trapeze

Gretna*

A young lady from Gretna Green
Crept into the vestry unseen
She pulled down her knickers
And likewise the vicars
And said, 'How's about it, old bean?'

Kirkcudbright

There was a chap from Kirkcudbright†
Whose bollocks were a sight to see
They were square not round
And each one weighed a pound
And on top of all that he had three

Lockerbie

A young lady to her chap from Lockerbie
Said, 'For once can't we just fuck properly?
Most people manage fun
Without sticking up their bum
A carrot or a stick of broccoli'

---

† Pronounced 'Kirk-koo-bree'

Locharbriggs

A young lady from Locharbriggs
Trained her vagina alone in her digs
So it could smoke cigarettes
Something that she regrets
Now each day it has three packs of cigs

Newton Stewart

A chap to his wife from Newton Stew-art
Said, 'Our love life most needs a kick start
At least put down that book
You're reading mid-fuck
Discourse on the Method‡ by René Descartes'

---

‡ This being one of the principal works by the 17th century French philosopher, René Descartes (pronounced 'Dae-cart', of course) or to give the book its full title *Discourse on the Method of Rightly Conducting One's Reason and of Seeking Truth in the Sciences* (or if she was reading it in the original French: *Discours de la méthode pour bien conduire sa raison, et chercher la vérité dans les sciences*)

Stranraer

There was a young man from Stranraer
Who had ambitions to be a porn star
He caused quite some fuss
At the Jobcentre Plus
Showing the asset that might take him far

East Ayrshire

Auchinleck

Once a prostitute from Auchinleck
Told me, 'Not you again, flippin' heck
I've already said it
I'm not offering credit
And I won't take a post-dated cheque'

Cumnock

At a church service one day in Cumnock
To the vicar I said, 'I don't want to mock
But it might be quite wise
To do up your flies
The congregation can see your cock'

Darvel

Said a cocky young fellow from Darvel
'My penis is one fucking marvel
It can shoot jets of semen
Out to sea like a demon
And I once hit the sails of a carvel†'

---

† A carvel, also known as a caravel, being a two- or three-masted sailing ship with a high poop deck as used by the Spanish and Portuguese in the 15th and 16th centuries. Quite what one of these was doing still being ocean-going at the time of the young man's claim is something that must remain a mystery.

Drongan

A freak accident happened in Drongan
When this chap's privates got dropped a gong on
The metal plate from the gong
Sliced off half of his dong
So now he has less of a long 'un

Dunlop

I found in the town of Dunlop
The stock was low in their sex shop
They had no bondage slings
Anal beads or cock rings
So I walked out the place in a strop

Galston

At Galston in the Valley of Irvine
I once ate a meal quite unnerving
The sausage gave me a shock
It looked just like my cock
Apart from its more pronounced curving

Kilmarnock

There was a young man from Kilmar-nock
With a strange manner of taking stock
On alternate Mondays
He'd check in his undies
To make sure he had two balls and a cock

Mauchline

A nudist from the town of Mauchline‡
Made a really quite horrible din
The day he caught his wiener
In the door of his Cortina
And it came out looking rather more thin

Stewarton

This prostitute from Stewar-ton
Had breasts that could not be outdone
I said, 'That's me banjaxed
I've already climaxed
And you've only just got out the one'

---

‡ Pronounced 'Moch-lin'

East Dunbartonshire

Bearsden

At A&E to a chap from Bearsden
They said, 'What is it this time, then?
We'll give you some verbal
If it's a bloody gerbil
You've got stuck up your arse once again'

Bishopbriggs

When I stayed in Bishopbriggs
I breakfasted on syrup of figs
But with results gruesome
When I felt my bowels loosen
A minute after leaving my digs

Cadder

I called on my lady friend from Cadder
To see me she couldn't be gladder
She said, 'I've been blue
With nothing to do
Quick, get out your trouser adder'

Kirkintilloch

On the day I was in Kirkintilloch
I ran to the top of a hillock
And got my knob out
And waved it about
It was said I behaved like a pillock

Lennoxtown

A young lady from Lennox-town
To her man said, 'This time please slow down
Unlike with most blokes
You're at your vinegar strokes
Before I've got my pants all the way down'

Lenzie

The pornography I bought once in Lenzie
Set me wanking away in a frenzy
It was so hardcore
I made my dick sore
And put it out of use till the next Wednesday

Milngavie

I rang up a little bit shy
The hotel I stayed at in Milngavie†
Saying 'I feel such a chump
I've left there my penis pump
Can I pick it up if I pass by?'

---

† Which is pronounced very differently from its spelling as 'Mil-guy'

Milton of Campsie

A young lady from Milton of Campsie
Said, 'For eagerness I am a champ, me
You scan skip the foreplay
Let's just have it away
My crotch it is already damp, see'

East Lothian

Cockenzie and Port Seton

With my girlfriend from the town of Port Seton
I finished it because she would cheat on
Me, with this feller
Who was far from stellar
But his penis had rather more meat on

Dunbar

At my stall at the fete in Dunbar
I sold jams and preserves by the jar
But the sales of little pots
Each containing two shots
Of my pearl jam didn't go very far

Haddington

I once met this lady from Haddington
Who said if I'd help her get her cladding done
She would let me see her bare
Which sounded quite fair
But she'd meant her old teddy bear, Paddington

Musselburgh

I met a young lady from Musselburgh
Who told me that I mustn't hustle her
But that it might arouse her
If I had in my trousers
A reasonably decent love muscle there

North Berwick

To his doctor a chap from North Berwick
Said, 'I like everything span and spick
But you've got to help me
This must be OCD
I twelve times a day clean my dick'

Prestonpans

I lost the job I had in Prestonpans
When I had to make some copies of plans
And to help the time pass
Photocopied my ass
And showed everybody the scans

Tranent

I went to a conference in Tranent
Which was quite a boring event
But for reasons obscure
I had thoughts impure
And sat with a big trouser tent

East Renfrewshire

Barrhead

There was a young man from Barrhead
Who kept several corpses in bed
Saying, 'My necrophilia
Is getting much sillier
I must find a live one instead'

Clarkston

When he broke wind a chap from Clarks-ton
Said, 'I'm sorry the smell is so strong
And a little bit eggy
But forgive me I beg ye
I've eaten a lot of foo yung'

Giffnock

The service at the tailors in Giffnock
Was so personal it gave me a shock
I was surprised to see
They found it necessa-ry
To measure the size of my cock

Neilston

There is a young man from Neil-ston
Who collects in jam jars just for fun
All of the jism
From his onanism
And to date he's filled seventy-one

Newton Mearns

An odd young man from Newton Mearns
Had a sexual thing for tea urns
Especially when hot
Which explains how he got
A penis with third degree burns

Falkirk

Bo'ness

At Tesco's in the town of Bo'ness
With, I might say, a degree of finesse
I was showing my chopper
To a fellow shopper
And she gave it a gentle caress

Bonnybridge

At the library in Bonnybridge
They said, 'Keep down your groaning a smidge'
I said, 'Sorry, my bitching
Is due to this itching
I've been bit on my balls by a midge'

Denny

There once was a young man from Denny
Who was born with a bollock too many
Though some people would scoff
He was much better off
Than his brother who hadn't got any

Falkirk

There was a young man from Falkirk
Whose penis one day went berserk
And came everywhere
With litres to spare
Then twitched with a curious jerk

Grangemouth

In Grangemouth there's an oil refinery
A port, a canal and a winery
And to thrill you to bits
All the girls have 10 tits
That is if you count them in binary

Hallglen

From the newsagents one day in Glen village
A young man did all their porn mags pillage
And left a note saying, 'Thanks
These'll be good for some wanks
And a fair amount of semen spillage'

Larbert

The young lady I met in Larbert
Had breasts that were lovely and pert
I told her as much
As she fondled my crutch
And I knew I was on a dead cert

Stenhousemuir

There was a chap from Stenhousemuir
Whose ejaculations were premature
Till he hit on this thing
To tie his balls up with string
And razor wire just to make sure

Fife

Anstruther

The girlfriend I once had from Anstruther†
Suggested thus that we be true to each other:
'I'll stop blowing the man
From the bakery van
If you agree to stop knobbing my mother'

---

† Which is pronounced with a short 'u' as in 'syrup' not a long
'u' as in 'truth'

Benarty

There was a pirate from Ben-arty
Who said to me, 'Ah ha me hearty
Well by any means
I enjoyed all those beans
But they've left me most terribly farty'

Buckhaven

At the town parade once in Buckhaven
I was cautioned for my misbehaving
It was such a nice day
I got carried away
And my dick in my hand I was waving

Burntisland

A naturist from Burntisland
Played piano nude in a jazz band
Till one sorry day
His knob was in the way
When the lid slammed on his baby grand

Cardenden

A couple from the town of Cardenden
Would have intercourse out in the garden then
Pop round to next door
To plead and implore
Their neighbours that they might pardon them

Cowdenbeath

There was a whore from Cowdenbeath
Who offered cheap oral relief
But despite the low price
You'd not come back twice
On account of her rather sharp teeth

Cupar

There was a young lady from Cupar
Who I thought was really quite super
Just one look down her blouse
Would have me aroused
And she'd wank me off into a stupor

Dalgety Bay

An old man from Dalgety Bay
Took his testicles round on a tray
Saying, 'Look at their size
I'm offering a prize
For the first one to guess what they weigh'

Dunfermline

A contest was held in Dunfermline
That the person pissing farthest would win
I surpassed the whole nation
At such urination
When my stream of piss reached Dublin

Ferry Port on Craig

With a young lady from Ferry Port on Craig
I said, 'I'm sorry my erection's so vague
I guess I shouldn't oughta
Have drunk all that porter
Not to mention that bottle of Haig'

Glenrothes

There was a chap from Glenrothes, Fife
Who bought himself a mail order wife
And though he wasn't fussy
She hadn't a pussy
And her cock gave him the shock of his life

High Valleyfield

With a dominatrix from High Valleyfield
For some pain and discomfort I steeled
Myself, but discovered
With my bum uncovered
Her whipping it rather appealed

Inverkeithing

To his butler a lord from Inverkeithing
Said, 'I've just given the maid a good beefing
I've still got the condom
On the end of my dong
Could you help me, please, with my unsheathing?'

Kelty

A young lady from the town of Kelty
Gave me a smile that would melt me
But I didn't expect
Her next move so direct
She stuck her hand down my trousers and felt me

Kirkcaldy

At the library one day in Kirkcaldy‡
I said to them, 'Oh lordy lordy
With *The Perfumed Garden*
I couldn't get one hard-on
Have you got something slightly more bawdy?'

---

‡ Pronounced 'Kirk-caw-dee'

Leslie

Said a chap from Leslie in Fife
'You should see the tits of my new wife
With that right pair of beauties
My husbandly duties
Will be a pleasure the rest of my life'

Leven

My landlady when I stayed in Leven
Had a chest that was massive and heaving
And when she let me get my hands
On her mammary glands
I found the sensation quite pleasing

Lochgelly

I met a dominatrix from Lochgelly
Who fair turned my knees into jelly
When she set about my cock
With a big lump of rock
My screams could be heard in New Delhi

Methil*

There was a young man from Methil
Who swallowed a dynamite pill
His heart retired
His bum backfired
And his willy shot over the hill

Newport-on-Tay

A young lady from Newport-on-Tay
Was quite the one for the foreplay
All through our luncheon
She stroked my love truncheon
Till the waiter said, 'Put it away'

Oakley

A chap caught me with his wife from Oakley
And announced he would happily choke me
But said, 'Don't stop mid-screw
I'll wait till you're through
Like that, I'm a reasonable bloke, me'

Rosyth

There once was a man from Rosyth
Who bought himself a mail order wife
But he regretted his punt
When he couldn't find her cunt
And her cock gave him the shock of his life

St. Andrews

At St. Andrews once on the golf course
My partner took a shot with such force
He clipped my meat and two veg
With the back swing of his wedge
For which he showed quite some remorse

Highland

Alness

With my new lady friend from Alness
I said, 'Must we be so adventur-ess?
Please call a physician
The last sexual position
Has left my knob in some distress'

Aviemore

There was a young man from Aviemore
Who said, 'I find doing housework a chore
But with mother calling round
I suppose time could be found
To clear those used rubber sheaths from the floor'

Culloden

I was feeling a little downtrodden
When I met this fair maid from Culloden
Who fancied me so much
It was affecting her crutch
And she told me her panties were sodden

Dingwall*

There was a young man from Dingwall
Whose arsehole was no good at all
When he sat down to poo
It went all askew
And shot all his shit up the wall

Fort William

To Fort William near to Glen Coe
I went once with plenty of dough
But met this high-class hooker
Who was such a fine looker
I blew all my cash in one go

Grantown-on-Spey

At my hotel in Grantown-on-Spey
I said, 'Your broadband again's gone astray
Ask if the porter Daz'll
Lend me one of his *Razzle*
So I can get my wanking back underway?'

Invergordon

In Invergordon where there was a mutiny†
Said a chap giving himself some scrutiny
'It's been many a year
Since I saw my dick, I fear
I must cut down on some of my gluttony'

---

† This is a reference to the Invergordon Mutiny of 1931 for
which the town is known. I'm also aware that
'mutiny'/'gluttony' is one of my more inventive rhymes.

Inverness

At the vicar's party in Inverness
The requirement was for fancy dress
But I caused quite a shock
Going dressed as a cock
And the evening was not a success

John o' Groats

There was a young man from John o' Groats
Who was yet to have his first oats
And at age thirty-three
Still had his virginity
Unless you count the times he fucked goats

Kingussie

There was a young lady from Kingussie‡
With an amazing musical pussy
It'd play for a starter
A Beethoven sonata
Then several works by Debussy

Nairn

I once went to the Nairn Jazz Festival
But found the event quite detestable
Especially when this chap
Dropped his sax in my lap
Which caught me just in the right testicle

---

‡ Which is pronounced 'King-ewsie' and therefore this limerick
may require a particular pronunciation of the word 'pussy'!

Skye

When I was on the Isle of Skye
I overdid the old Spanish fly
I had a stiff member
From the fourth of December
Till Friday the tenth of July

Tain

I found out in the small town of Tain
Sexual practice was far from mundane
One particular group
Formed a curious loop
That I understand is called a monk's chain

Thurso

One winter in the town of Thurso
When bleak weather was in full flow
A notice was composed:
'The public toilets are closed
So watch out for much yellow snow'

Tobermory

The night that I stayed in Tobermory
It was a varied political story
I early on kissed
A Scottish Nationalist
But then shagged a Green and a Tory

Wick

There once was a young man from Wick
Who could give his own penis a lick
At most social functions
He'd have no compunction
About showing the party this trick

Inverclyde and Glasgow

Glasgow

There was a young lady Glaswegian
Who was famed for her pubic region
Her twat was so huge
It became a refuge
And an outpost for the French Foreign Legion

Gourock

There was a young man from Gourock
Who went out wearing only a sock
Saying, 'You must conclude
That I'm not really nude
When I'm wearing the sock on my cock'

Greenock

I called on my lady friend from Green-ock
And she said to me, 'How have you been, cock?
Now that you've called round
Quick get your trousers down
It's been at least two days since I've seen cock'

Inverkip

A young lady from Inverkip
Would give hand jobs at quite a fast clip
And would finish most blokes
With a few lightning strokes
Before you could say, 'Toodle pip!'

Kilmacolm

A sculptor from Kilmacolm†
Sold garden ornaments from his home
But he didn't sell a lotta
The one in terracotta
Of a bullfrog giving head to a gnome

---

† Pronounced 'Kil-ma-coam'

Port Glasgow

In mid-screw a wife from Port Glasgow
To her husband said, 'You are so slow
I've nearly finished this book
That I started reading mid-fuck
And it's a long one by Jean-Jacques Rousseau‡'

Wemyss Bay

A young lady to her chap from Wemyss Bay
Said, 'Our lovemaking's got a little passé
I'm going to go ask our neighbours
What positions they favour
With a door-to-door sexual survey'

---

‡ The 18th century Genevan philosopher whose political
philosophy influenced the French Revolution

Midlothian and Edinburgh

Bonnyrigg

There was a young lady from Bonnyrigg
Who was very fond of having a frig
With dildoes by the number
Or courgette or cucumber
Or anything phallic and big

Dalkeith

There once was a whore from Dalkeith
Who was so accomplished at hand relief
That whatever you'd planned
You'd come in her hand
Before you got near her curtains of beef

Edinburgh

A man from Edinburgh, Scotland's capital
Went for forty days without a crap at all
Then when he went to the loo
He produced so much poo
The toilet bowl didn't quite trap it all

Gorebridge

In Gorebridge the home of gunpowder
They served me with this onion chowder
That led me to commence
On such flatulence
I don't think I've broken wind louder

Kirkliston

With my lady friend from Kirkliston
I said, 'My dear, I hope you won't insist on
Lovemaking tonight
My erection's too slight
'Cause of all of the gin I've got pissed on'

Loanhead

To the dominatrix I knew from Loanhead
I said, 'Yes, please do take me to bed
But this time please promise
Not to whack my John Thomas
With that length of piping made of lead'

Penicuik

There was a young man from Penicuik†
Who had once read a medical book
And although he'd insist
'I'm no gynaecologist'
He'd be happy to take a good look

---

† Pronounced 'Pennycook'

Queensferry

'This evening,' said a lady from Queensferry
'Could you stand in for my husband Terry?
The chances are slim
Of an erection from him
After he's drunk two bottles of sherry'

Moray

Buckie

While stood at a urinal in Buckie
A man said to me, 'Excuse me, ducky
That dick in your hand
Looks rather grand
In comparison I feel quite unlucky'

Cullen

There was a young fellow from Cullen
Whose love life was a bit of a dull 'un
'Cause he found both too lewd
He never wanked or screwed
So his ball sac was rather a full 'un

Dipple

A young lady I met from Dipple
Excitement, she caused quite a ripple
She had such lovely tits
I was thrilled to bits
Just at the sight of one nipple

Elgin

There was a young lady from El-gin
Who thought sex would be a mortal sin
But if no one was looking
She'd think nothing of fucking
Herself with a big rolling pin

Forres

Said a husband to his wife from Forres
'I've read your magazines again, Doris
But I'm not really a fan
Of *Cosmopoli-tan*
And what's the thing they call a cli-toris?'

Keith

At my job interview in the town of Keith
For my attire they gave me some grief
And said I just shouldn't wear
A T-shirt with a tear
Or with a crudely drawn penis motif

Lossiemouth

In Lossiemouth on the River Lossie
A young man whene'er at a loss, he
Would brush his pubic hair
With patience and care
In the hope that it would keep it glossy

MORAY

Portknockie

One day when I was in Portknockie
We were playing a game of field hockey
When the ball, if you please
Caught me in the testes
And my screams could be heard in Milwaukie

North Ayrshire

Ardrossan

A miserly chap from Ardrossan
Saved up all the sperm from his tossing
To use it as glue
And saved pubic hairs too
For later use for dental flossing

Beith

They staged a biblical play once in Beith
But the costumes were a little too brief
The end of Adam's wang
Did quite clearly hang
Out from under his tiny fig leaf

Dalry

The meal that I ate in Dalry†
With food standards did not quite comply
And I felt rather sick
When I found a sheep's dick
In the middle of my cold shepherd's pie

---

† Pronounced 'Dall-rye'

Irvine

A widowed old lady from Irvine
Thought her husband's dick worth preserving
And even went as far
As to display it in a jar
Which her house guests found somewhat unnerving

Kilbirnie

A doctor and nurse from Kilbirnie
Were seen having sex on a gurney‡
When it wheeled away
Through the streets for a day
Which was quite an incredible journey

---

‡ Which, in case a definition is required, is a light bed on
wheels, used to move patients in a hospital

Kilwinning

By the time I reached the town of Kilwinning
I'd been through an A to Z of sinning
Without anything new
There was fuck all else to do
Than to start again at the beginning

Largs

In Largs at the Barrfields Pavilion
I once met an old vaudevillian
Whose mind reading trick
Was from the audience to pick
Out all the women who'd had a Brazilian

Saltcoats*

There was a young lady from Saltcoats
Who had sex with twenty-five goats
And when she was through
She had a cold brew
And wrote them all nice thank you notes

Stevenson

There was a young man from Stevenson
Who prayed thus one Friday at Evensong:
'Lord, don't think me grumpy
But my dick's rough and lumpy
Could you grant me a more smooth and even dong?'

NORTH AYRSHIRE

West Kilbride

An exhibitionist from West Kilbride
Went for a naked hang-glide
Which only went wrong
When he caught his dong
On a pylon that he hadn't spied

North Lanarkshire

Airdrie

There was a young man from Airdrie
Who was bit on his dick by a flea
His date that night was botched
As he scratched at his crotch
And wailed like a howling banshee

Bellshill

At this awful restaurant in Bellshill
The waiter asked what to do with the bill
But he said my suggestion
Was out of the question
As he'd another one stuck up there still

Chryston

A chap to his wife from Chryston
Said, 'My dear, must you insist on
Frigging yourself away
For the whole of the day
Your finger's in and out like a piston'

Cleland

To her husband said a wife from Cleland
'Romantic music whilst we screw would be grand
But I will not assent
To this live accompaniment
By the Clackmannon District Brass Band'

Coatbridge

There was a young man from Coatbridge
Who got himself locked in a fridge
By half ten that night
His dick had frostbite
And his bollocks had shrunk by a smidge

Cumbernauld

There was a young man from Cumbernauld
Whose manners were quite uncontrolled
He once got out his pecker
On a crowded double decker
And shouted out, 'Who wants a hold?'

Harthill

Said a chap to his wife from Harthill
'Our love life is going downhill
And laughing like a hyena
At the sight of my wiener
Is making things rather worse still'

Kilsyth

A father from the town of Kilsyth
Said, 'I may have ruined my boy's chances for life
That DIY circumcision
Was a stupid decision
Especially with this rather blunt knife'

Moodiesburn

With a young lady from Moodiesburn
I said, 'Your offer of sex I must spurn
The fact's inescapable
I'm no longer capable
After drinking nine pints of Sauternes†'

---

† Sauternes being a sweet French wine, pronounced 'saw-tern'

Motherwell

At a second hand shop in Motherwell
A sports jacket they tried to me sell
Saying, 'It's a bargain find
That is if you don't mind
The semen stain on the lapel'

Overtown

A friend of mine from Over-town
Was oddly dressed when I popped round
And I just had to ask
'Why are you wearing a basque
Hot pants and a beauty queen's crown?'

Plains

At a shop in the village of Plains
Over choices a shopper took pains
Saying, 'Persil, Daz or Bold
Please can I be told
Which works best on tough semen stains?'

Shotts

With this young lady from the town of Shotts
We tried screwing in various spots
Then she said, 'Would it suit ya
To work through the *Kama Sutra*
Till we tie ourselves up in some knots?'

Wishaw

The tailor in the town of Wishaw
Advised me as I walked in the door
'The shape of your dobber
I can see through your clobber
Those trousers are too tight for sure'

Perth and Kinross

Auchterarder

A young lady from Auchterarder
Said to her chap, 'Can't you get your dick harder?
Forget this for a screw
I'd rather make do
With that courgette I found in the larder'

Blairgowrie and Rattray

I was spurned by this lady from Rattray
Despite my best efforts at flattery
She said, 'See you later
I'd prefer my vibrator
Even with its slightly flat battery'

Crieff

A masochist from the small town of Crieff
Said, 'It might be your idea of grief
But I'm glad I eschewed
Swimming trunks and swam nude
And chafed my dick on that rough coral reef'

Killiecrankie

A young lady from Killiecrankie
Was dead keen for some hanky panky
She aroused me so surely
I came prematurely
And alas she got really quite cranky

Kinross

The pornography I bought from Kinross
Was frankly an utter dead loss
It was hardly top drawer
And very softcore
And I couldn't even manage one toss

Perth

When in Perth on the River Tay
I went to a BDSM soirée
And despite my complaints
Their bondage restraints
Left my balls aching all the next day

Scone

I went shopping with a young lady from Scone†
Who gave hand jobs most inopportune
I said, 'Please be more discrete
With my trouser meat
At least wait till we're out of Monsoon‡'

---

† Pronounced 'Skoon'
‡ The retail women's clothing chain with shops worldwide and in a number of Scottish towns and cities

Renfrewshire

Bishopton

At a masochists' party in Bishop-ton
Not being one to be easily outdone
When a chap got out his dick
And whacked it with a stick
I got out mine and shot it with a gun

Bridge of Weir

At a brothel I found in Bridge of Weir
I complained the hand jobs were severe:
'Your young lady Cilla
Has the grip of a gorilla
And has done me a mischief I fear'

Eaglesham

With a young lady from Eagle-sham
At a kebab shop she said to me, 'Damn
I swear on my honour
That badly packed donner
Looks just like my own bearded clam'

Erskine

A masochist from the town of Erskine
Said, whilst we chatted over a gin
'My idea of Nirvana
Is a tank of piranha
That I like to let my dick dangle in'

Houston

Said a young lady from Houston:
'I must clean that sofa I was seduced on
And after doing that
Everything else in the flat
That my lover and I have love juiced on'

Johnstone

There was a young chef from Johnstone
Who was terribly accident prone
He gave himself some cuts
And sliced off both his nuts
When a chicken he was trying to debone

Linwood

Said a dashing young man from Linwood:
'I'm disappointed with my manhood
I thought wearing chiffon
Might give me a stiff on
But I see that it still hasn't stood'

Paisley

I was caught by this fellow from Paisley
In the act fucking his wife like crazy
But he said, 'Here's ten bob
You've saved me a job
I'd screw her myself but I'm lazy'

Renfrew

Said a young man who came from Renfrew
'This bestiality I must eschew
My last three girlfriends
All had very nice ends
But all had four legs and went moo'

Scottish Borders

Coldstream

There was a young man from Coldstream
Whose carelessness was quite extreme
Whilst brushing in haste
He confused his toothpaste
With his grandfather's haemorrhoid cream

Duns

There once was a young man from Duns
Whose balls were like two Chelsea buns
But if their size was impressive
Their weight was excessive
As each one weighed nearly two tons

Eyemouth

In Eyemouth, the famed fishing port
I was surprised at the things that I caught
A dose of chlamydia
From this young lady Lydia
The crabs and a large penile wart

Galashiels

Once two brothers from Galashiels
Were put through some dreadful ordeals
By a dominatrix
Who stamped on their pricks
Then did it again in high heels

Hawick

In Hawick in the Scottish Borders
There's a club of *Razzle* magazine hoarders
Who collect every issue
And wrap them in tissue
And wank over them in different orders

Innerleithen

An old weaver from Innerleithen
Had a foible that will take some believin'
He would always depict
The image of his dick
In each and every piece of his weaving

Jedburgh

Announced the local radio reporter:
'There's contest in Jedburgh on Jed Water
Where they'll award a gold gong
For the longest dong
And a silver for the one slightly shorter'

Kelso

I stripped naked one night in Kelso
And ran round to put on a show
First preparing my knob
With a fairly big blob
Of fluorescent paint to make it glow

Newtown St. Boswells

A young man from Newton St. Boswells
On the end of his dick, tied some bells
Which chimed to perfection
When he got an erection
And CDs of the tunes he now sells

Peebles

From my night out in Peebles, Borders
I recall well the bar at last orders
But I just don't remember
What I did with my member
That got me served with three court orders

Selkirk

There was a young man from Selkirk
With quite an odd physical quirk
Whenever he'd see
A nice cup of tea
His penis would suddenly perk

St. Abbs

In a takeaway a maid from St. Abbs
Suddenly pointed at one of their kebabs
And said, 'That's uncanny
It looks just like my fanny
Apart from it hasn't got crabs'

Shetland and Orkney

Kirkwall

There was a young man from Kirkwall
Who had quite a terrible fall
On some very sharp rock
Which sliced off his cock
And left him too missing a ball

Lerwick*

There was once a girl from Lerwick
Who said to her mum, 'What's a dick?'
She said, 'My dear Annie,
It goes in your fanny
And jumps up and down till it's sick'

Stromness

There was a young lady from Stromness, Orkney
Who set about trying to stalk me
But she needed no persistence
As I put up no resistance
And quite easily would let her pork me

South Ayrshire

Ayr

There once was a young man from Ayr
Whose sex doll had real pubic hair
But whilst at her furry cup
He'd have to blow her up
As she needed a puncture repair

Girvan

To the National Trust, a chap from Girvan
Wrote of a cause, he said, most deserving:
'Of my dick get a measure
It's a national treasure
Could you send me funds for its preserving?'

Maybole

A boastful gentleman from Maybole
Said, 'I am rather proud of my pole
There was no bigger phallus
In *Debbie Does Dallas*
And I really deserved a star role'

Prestwick

There was a young man from Prestwick
Who always came a little too quick
Till in measures quite drastic
He tied his balls with elastic
And used dry ice to numb up his dick

Troon*

There was a young man from Troon
Whose farts could be heard on the moon
When least you'd expect 'em
They'd burst from his rectum
With the force of a raging typhoon

South Lanarkshire

Blantyre

Whist in the town of Blantyre
I went to an auction sale that was dire
Where they tried to dispose
Of some melted dildoes
Which stock had been damaged by fire

Bothwell

A sales manageress from Bothwell
Would bed all her male personnel
But if sales were really up
She'd drink from the furry cup
And bed all the women as well

Cambuslang

At a pyjama party in Cambuslang
I had not meant to show off my wang
But as we caroused
I got slightly aroused
And out of my 'jamas it sprang

Carluke

Said a boastful young man from Carluke
'I may not be a lord or a duke
But I've blessed with a dong
So uncommonly long
It must be a biological fluke'

East Kilbride

There was a chap from East Kilbride
Who was caught with his bit on the side
He was asked by his wife
Who was holding a knife
'Do you want your balls grilled or fried?'

Elsrickle

With a lady friend from Elsrickle
I found myself in a bit of a pickle
I upset her quite surely
When I came prematurely
When she gave my dick just a quick tickle

Hamilton

There was a farmer from Hamil-ton
Who when he'd slayed a pig, waste he would shun
He'd eat every part
From its kidneys to heart
And its dick in a frankfurter bun

Kirkmuirhill

There was a young man from Kirkmuirhill
Who for an electrical thrill
Put some serious wattage
Through his gentleman's sausage
And I hear that it's vibrating still

Lanark

There was a big explosion in Lanark
One bonfire night just after dark
When a flatulent chap
Suffered quite a mishap
When his farts were lit by a stray spark

Larkhall

At the fete in the town of Larkhall
A big hit was my sexual aids stall
Demand was so fantastic
For the vaginas in plastic
It just ended up in a brawl

Law

There was a young lady from Law
Who I once did as follows implore:
'If your answer is nay
To a roll in the hay
What do you think to a fuck in the straw?'

Lesmahagow

A human cannonball from Lesma-hagow
Said, 'Light the touch paper when I say, "go"
But the explosion went wrong
And blew off his dong
And his balls landed in San Diego

Rutherglen

There was a young lady from Rutherglen
For whom sex had been beyond her ken
Till she met an instructor
Who taught her and fucked her
And she couldn't get enough of it then

Stonehouse

I lived for a while in Stonehouse
And my mother called round and did grouse:
'You should clean for sure
All this dust from the floor
Not to mention this dead pubic louse'

Strathaven

One fine day in the town of Strathaven‡
I did some chalk art on the paving
But a bye-law I infringed
When I drew a hairy minge
Not to mention two more that were shaven

---

‡ Pronounced 'Stray-ven'

Uddingston

In Uddingston by the banks of the Clyde
At a brothel I was beckoned inside
They said, 'Don't be nervous
We'll provide a nice service
For your trouser snake that's one-eyed'

Stirling

Bannockburn

A financial adviser from Bannockburn
To his client said, 'Will you not learn?
A sex doll indestructible
Is not tax deductible
Remove it from your tax return'

Callander

There was a young lady from Callander
With a mixed blessing mammary glandular
The size of her tits
Would thrill her to bits
But they were shaped a little rectangular

Dunblane

Said a mother to her son in Dunblane:
'My Ann Summers catalogue has a new stain
And furthermore, Trevor
Pages are stuck together
Have you wanked over this yet again?'

Stirling

There was a young lady from Stirling
Who could set her nipples a-twirling
For this trick with her tits
She'd charge you two bits
Or thirty-five pence in pounds sterling

West Dunbartonshire

Alexandria

I spilt beer one night in Alexandria
In the lap of my lady friend, Andrea
Who said, 'Oh you big prat
I'll go dry off my twat
With a quick handstand under the hand dryer†'

---

† I'm aware that Alexandria/Andrea/hand dryer may be one of
my more inventive sets of rhymes.

Balloch

There was a young man from Bal-loch
Who gained a stiffness in his cock
At an angle quite steep
If he thought of a sheep
And upright if he thought of a flock

Bonhill

There was a young man from Bonhill
Who at wanking had particular skill
And wrote a dissertation
On the art of masturbation
That got him an Oxford D.Phil‡

---

‡ D.Phil, rather than PhD, being the term for a doctorate used
by Oxford University

Bowling

I met a young lady in Bowling
Who was doing some opinion polling
I said she got my vote
And she fondled my scrote
And soon in the hay we were rolling

Clydebank

There was an artist from Clydebank
Who died with nothing in the bank
And left as an estate
Just a few self-portraits
Each depicting him having a wank

Dumbarton*

A flatulent actor from Dumbarton
Led a life exceedingly spartan
Till a playwright one day
Wrote a well-received play
With a part for the actor to fart in

West Lothian

Armadale

There was a young man from Armadale
With flatulence on an industrial scale
Who could emit from his ass
So much methane gas
It could well replace fracking for shale

Bathgate

There was a young man from Bathgate
Who went fishing with his dick as bait
An idea unwise
But to his surprise
He caught four eels, a cod and a skate

Broxburn

There once was young man from Broxburn
Who at a whorehouse was waiting in turn
When he spotted his mother
Who was serving another
Which gave him a spot of concern

East Calder

A young lady I met in East Calder
Had an approach that couldn't be bolder
She said, 'Oh, you'll do
Give me a quick screw
Before I get very much older'

Fauldhouse

At the doctor's surgery in Fauldhouse
I said, 'Could you look here at this pubic louse?
With my pubes a refuge
It has grown quite so huge
It is nearly the size of a mouse'

Linlithgow

With this young lady in Linlithgow
My performance was quite a poor show
My dick wouldn't rise
But it had been unwise
To first drink five pints of Bordeaux

Livingston

Once in the town of Living-ston
I went to a beauty salon
But wanted my money back
On their back, sac and crack
As they'd left half my pubic hair on

Stoneyburn

At the sex shop once in Stoneyburn
They asked me to do them a good turn
And test two plastic vaginas
To say which was finer
But the difference I found hard to discern

West Calder

A young lady I met in West Calder
Could frankly not have been bolder
She wore a big badge
That said, 'I've got a nice vag
And your cock I wanna get holda'

Whitburn

There was a young lady from Whitburn
Who once had a peculiar turn
At the botanical garden
She said, 'I beg your pardon'
Then pissed on their fragrant wood fern

Western Isles

Western Isles*

A boatman from the Western Isles
Suffered severely from piles
He couldn't sit down
Without a deep frown
So he had to row standing for miles

Harris

There once was a young man from Harris
Who cast his dick in plaster of paris
He put it on a stand
And thought it looked grand
On the dashboard of his Toyota Yaris

Stornoway

With this lass in the town of Stornoway
Something happened to quite take my horn away
I had a mishap
With my Arab strap
Which left half my pubic hair torn away

Uist

Waking early one day in Uist
I fancied a quick one off the wrist
But I didn't come soon
And when it got to noon
I decided I'd better desist

Index of Towns

A
Aberdeen, 1
Airdrie, 94
Alexandria, 135
Alloa, 21
Alness, 65
Alva, 22
Annan, 25
Anstruther, 53
Arbroath, 12
Ardrossan, 88
Armadale, 139
Auchinleck, 31
Auchterarder, 102
Aviemore, 66
Ayr, 120

B
Balloch, 136
Ballingry – see Benarty
Banchory, 2
Banff, 2
Bannockburn, 132
Barrhead, 45
Bathgate, 140
Bearsden, 36
Beith, 89
Bellshill, 95
Benarty, 54
Bishopbriggs, 37
Bishopton, 106
Blairgowrie and Rattray, 103

Blantyre, 123
Bo'ness, 48
Bonhill, 136
Bonnybridge, 49
Bonnyrigg, 78
Bothwell, 124
Bowling, 137
Brechin, 13
Bridge of Weir, 107
Broxburn, 140
Buckhaven, 54
Buckie, 83
Burntisland, 55

C

Cadder, 37
Callander, 133
Cambuslang, 124
Campbeltown, 17
Cardenden, 55
Carluke, 125
Carnoustie, 13
Castle Douglas, 26
Chryston, 95
Clackmannan, 22
Clarkston, 46
Cleland, 96
Clydebank, 137
Coatbridge, 96
Cockenzie and Port Seton, 41
Coldstream, 111
Cowdenbeath, 56
Crieff, 103
Cullen, 84
Culloden, 66

Cumbernauld, 97
Cumnock, 32
Cupar, 56

D
Dalbeattie, 26
Dalgety Bay, 57
Dalkeith, 79
Dalry, 89
Darvel, 32
Denny, 49
Dingwall, 67
Dipple, 84
Drongan, 33
Dumbarton, 138
Dumfries, 27
Dunbar, 42
Dunblane, 133
Dundee, 14
Dunfermline, 57
Dunlop, 33
Dunoon, 18
Duns, 112
Dyce, 3

E
Eaglesham, 107
East Calder, 141
East Kilbride, 125
Edinburgh, 79
Elgin, 85
Ellon, 3
Elsrickle, 126
Erskine, 108

Eyemouth, 112

F
Falkirk, 50
Fauldhouse, 141
Ferry Port on Craig, 58
Forfar, 14
Forres, 85
Fort William, 67
Fraserburgh, 4

G
Galashiels, 113
Galston, 34
Giffnock, 46
Girvan, 121
Glasgow, 74
Glenrothes, 58
Gorebridge, 80
Gourock, 75
Grangemouth, 50
Grantown-on-Spey, 68
Greenock, 75
Gretna, 27

H
Haddington, 42
Hallglen, 51
Hamilton, 126
Harris, 146
Harthill, 97
Hawick, 113
Helensburgh, 18
High Valleyfield, 59

Houston, 108
Huntly, 4

I
Innerleithen, 114
Inveraray, 19
Invergordon, 68
Inverkeithing, 59
Inverkip, 76
Inverness, 69
Inverurie, 5
Irvine, 90

J
Jedburgh, 114
John o' Groats, 69
Johnstone, 109

K
Keith, 86
Kelso, 115
Kelty, 60
Kemnay, 5
Kilbirnie, 90
Killiecrankie, 104
Kilmacolm, 76
Kilmarnock, 34
Kilsyth, 98
Kilwinning, 91
Kingswells, 6
Kingussie, 70
Kinross, 104
Kintore, 6
Kirkcaldy, 60

Kirkcudbright, 28
Kirkintilloch, 38
Kirkliston, 80
Kirkmuirhill, 127
Kirkwall, 118
Kirriemuir, 15

L
Lanark, 127
Larbert, 51
Largs, 91
Larkhall, 128
Law, 128
Lennoxtown, 38
Lenzie, 39
Lerwick, 119
Leslie, 61
Lesmahagow, 129
Leven, 61
Linlithgow, 142
Linwood, 109
Livingston, 142
Loanhead, 81
Locharbriggs, 29
Lochgelly, 62
Lochgilphead, 19
Lochore - see Benarty
Lockerbie, 28
Lossiemouth, 86

M
Macduff, 7
Mauchline, 35
Maybole, 121

Methil, 62
Milngavie, 39
Milton of Campsie, 40
Monifieth, 15
Montrose, 16
Moodiesburn, 98
Motherwell, 99
Muckhart, 23
Musselburgh, 43

N
Nairn, 70
Neilston, 47
Newport-on-Tay, 63
Newton Mearns, 47
Newton Stewart, 29
Newtonhill, 7
Newtown St. Boswells, 115
North Berwick, 43

O
Oakley, 63
Oban, 20
Oldmeldrum, 8
Overtown, 99

P
Paisley, 110
Peebles, 116
Penicuik, 81
Perth, 105
Peterculter, 8
Peterhead, 9

Plains, 100
Port Glasgow, 77
Portknockie, 87
Portlethen, 9
Prestonpans, 44
Prestwick, 122

Q
Queensferry, 82

R
Rattray, Perth and Kinross - see Blairgowrie and Rattray
Renfrew, 110
Rosyth, 64
Rothesay, 20
Rutherglen, 129

S
Saltcoats, 92
Scone, 105
Selkirk, 116
Shotts, 100
Skye, 71
South Queensferry - see Queensferry
St. Abbs, 117
St. Andrews, 64
Stenhousemuir, 52
Steornabhagh – see Stornoway
Stevenson, 92
Stewarton, 35
Stirling, 134
Stobswell, 16
Stonehaven, 10
Stonehouse, 130

Stoneyburn, 143
Stornoway, 146
Stranraer, 30
Strathaven, 130
Stromness, 119

T
Tain, 71
Tayport - see Ferry Port on Craig
Thurso, 72
Tillicoultry, 23
Tobermory, 72
Tranent, 44
Troon, 122
Tullibody, 24
Turriff, 10

U
Uddingston, 131
Uist, 147

W
Wemyss Bay, 77
West Calder, 143
West Kilbride, 93
Western Isles, 145
Westhill, 11
Whitburn, 144
Wick, 73
Wishaw, 101

ACKNOWLEDGEMENTS

Although none of them can or should be blamed for any of the limericks that appear here, a huge debt of thanks is owed to Jennifer Manson, Sarah Loving and Kevin Cross for all their help in various aspects of bringing this book to print.